# contents

# introduction

# WOODEN CHRISTMAS ORNAMENTS CROSS-STITCH KIT

## Instructions and Patterns

*Text and Patterns by*

**Sosae and Dennis Caetano**

RP **MINIS**

PHILADELPHIA

RP Minis®
Hachette Book Group
1290 Avenue of the Americas, New York, NY 10104
www.runningpress.com
@Running_Press

First Edition: September 2025

Published by RP Minis, an imprint of Hachette Book Group, Inc. The RP Minis name and logo is a registered trademark of Hachette Book Group, Inc.

Contact specialmarkets@hbgusa.com regarding special discounts for bulk purchases.

The publisher is not responsible for websites (or their content) that are not owned by the publisher.

Design by Susan Van Horn
Pine tree art provided by Getty Images Plus, credit Little_Airplane

ISBN: 979-8-89414-059-9

Made in Dongguan, China (HKD) 05/25 #01

'Tis the season for all things merry and bright . . . and crafty! Deck the halls with your very own handmade cross-stitch ornaments, and for a bonus touch of cheer, make them to give as gifts!

In this kit, you'll find everything you need to stitch three wooden cross-stitch ornaments from six festive designs: Ho Ho Ho, Cozy Cottage, Christmas Tree, Merry Wreath, Stripey Stocking, and Joy. Included in this kit are threads in bright red, fresh green, golden yellow, icy blue, and snowy white. Also included are two tapestry needles, three wooden cross-stitch ornament canvases, three pieces of ribbon for hanging, and of course, this mini book of instructions and patterns!

If you're new to cross-stitch, read through for a complete introduction on how to thread your needle and how to make those pretty little *x*-stitches. Be sure to check out the Finishing Touches and Helpful Tips sections to learn how to turn your cross-stitch into polished and pretty ornaments.

Cross-stitch is the ultimate cozy craft, so grab this nifty kit and a hot cup of cocoa and curl up on the couch in your favorite flannel pajamas. Choose your three favorite designs and start stitching your merry masterpieces!

# CROSS-STITCH BASICS

Cross-stitch is a particular style of embroidery, one in which you'll use a relatively blunt needle—called a tapestry needle—to sew x-shaped stitches onto your wooden canvas, creating a picture (in our case, a very Christmassy one). Here are a few basics to get you started!

## SUPPLIES

One of the benefits of cross-stitch is how easy it is to get started—you'll only need a few tools to begin working. With a wooden cross-stitch canvas, tapestry needles, threads, ribbons, and a pair of scissors, you'll have everything you need to create a holly jolly set of ornaments.

## *Wooden Canvas*

Included in this kit are three wooden cross-stitch canvases. They have pre-made holes that form a grid, which perfectly matches any of the six festive designs included in this kit.

## Needles

For any kind of embroidery project, you'll need a needle to pull your thread through the fabric, or in this case, the wooden canvas. With cross-stitch, the best tool is a tapestry needle, which has a dull tip. (Since the wooden canvas has pre-made holes, the needle doesn't have to be sharp.) There are two needles included in this kit—you only need one while you work, but it doesn't hurt to have an extra on hand.

## *Thread*

Thread is the most important, and the most fun, part of your cross-stitch tool kit. All of the patterns in this book use embroidery floss, which is a type of six-stranded thread that is especially well-suited to cross-stitch. (When you stitch, you will only use two strands at once. More on that later!) Included are five skeins of thread that correspond with the patterns in this book.

### *Scissors*

A pair of regular scissors will do in a pinch, but an extra-sharp pair of embroidery scissors will come in handy if you need to remove any stitches or get into small areas. Always be careful when using embroidery scissors.

## LET'S GET STITCHIN'

Once you've selected your favorite yuletide design, you're ready to begin. The first step is to thread your needle. To do so, first find the color that you'd like to start stitching with and cut a piece of thread that is roughly 18 inches long. You'll then want to separate your piece of thread into strands. (Each piece of embroidery thread is made up of six distinct strands, though you'll only want to use two at a time when stitching.) Gently pull two strands away from the remaining four, being careful not to knot them up. Once they are separated, put the remaining four strands aside for use later. Snip the ends of the two strands you'll be working with to give you a crisp edge for loading the needle. Feed the strands into the eye of the needle, leaving a short "tail" on one side (4 inches is good). Don't knot the thread!

## *Making Cross-Stitches*

The designs in this book use a method called "counted cross-stitch," meaning that you will base your stitches off of a pattern. With this type of pattern, you'll count the number of stitches in the color you're using and then make those stitches on your wooden canvas. You can work from the center outward, one row at a time, or one color at a time—it's up to you!

Once you've decided where to start, you can begin making stitches.

## MAKING SINGLE STITCHES

1. Pull your thread up through the small hole at the **bottom left** corner of your starting square, being sure to leave a 1-inch "tail" of floss on

the underside. Hold on to that tail as you make your next few stitches right on top of it—you'll want the back side of your stitches to cover the tail, securing it in place.

2. Pull the thread up through the canvas and then sew through the **top right** corner of the same square, creating a diagonal stitch. Pull your thread through to the back, taking care not to pull it too tightly—your goal should be stitches that are snug but not too tight. This is the first half of your stitch.

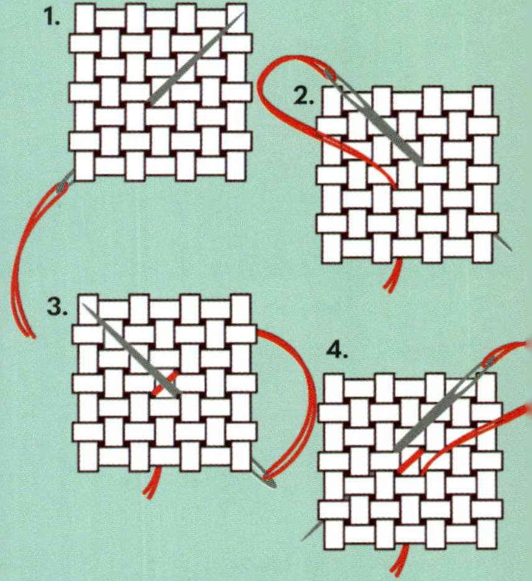
1.
2.
3.
4.

3. To create the second half of your stitch, sew up from the back of the canvas—through the **bottom right** corner of the square—to the front.
4. Pull your thread relatively taut, and then cross the square diagonally, sewing down through the **top left** hole. This will create the x shape of your cross-stitch.
5. Continue by making a stitch in the **bottom left** corner of the square next to your completed stitch. This square borders your first stitch, and shares two holes with it.

## MAKING A ROW OF STITCHES

1. To stitch a row in the same color, create the first half of each of the stitches by repeating steps 1 and 2 from the previous list, moving from left to right until you've created a row of diagonal lines all going from **bottom left** to **top right**.
2. When you reach the end of the row, bring your needle up through the **bottom right** hole and work your way back across, completing the *x* shape of each square as you go.

1.

2.

## *Finishing Touches*

Once you've finished stitching your wooden cross-stitch ornament, you can loop the ribbon through the hang-hole at the top of the canvas.

But if you want to give your ornament a more polished look, you can add felt backing first. (An added bonus of felt backing is that it hides and secures the stitches on the back of your ornament. This keeps stitches from coming loose or undone, as sometimes happens with wooden canvas.)

Felt fabric sheets are available at most craft stores and online. Choose colors that will complement your ornament, such as white, red, or green. (You may want to hold your ornament against a few pieces before you decide to make sure you're happy with how the felt will show through the holes.) When you've finished cross-stitching, place your ornament onto the felt sheet and gently trace around the diameter. Cut out the felt circle, making sure to notch the top portion to accommodate the hang-hole. Apply a very thin coat of all-purpose craft glue to the felt. (An old paintbrush works well for this.) Then adhere the felt to the back of the ornament. Press firmly and let dry for two hours. Alternatively, you can purchase felt with adhesive backing, which eliminates the need for craft glue. Trace and cut the felt before peeling off the paper on the adhesive side of the felt. Then apply it to the back of the ornament and press firmly to adhere.

## Helpful Tips

- *For a polished look, make all your stitches in the same direction and order: from the bottom left to the top right, and then the bottom right to the top left.*
- *Stitching on a wooden canvas is different from stitching on the aida fabric normally used for cross-stitch. Make your stitches slightly looser when stitching on wood, as wood has no "give." This will also make your stitches look fuller and prettier.*

- *If you find yourself wanting to buy additional thread so you can stitch these patterns again and again in the future, the DMC colors are:*
    - Bright red: DMC-666
    - Fresh green: DMC-702
    - Golden yellow: DMC-973
    - Icy blue: DMC-964
    - Snowy white: DMC-5200

# PATTERNS

## HO HO HO

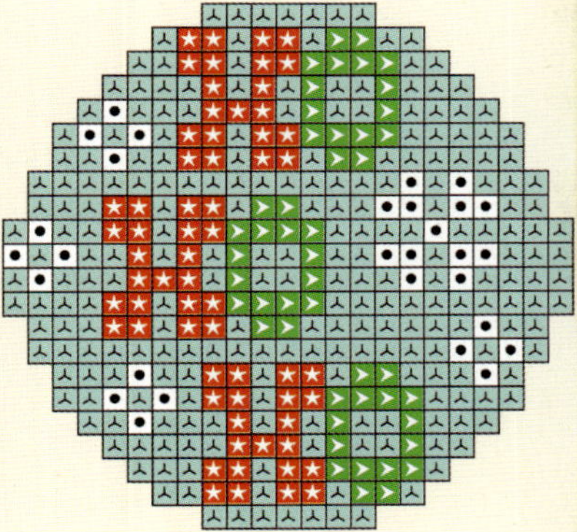

# COZY COTTAGE

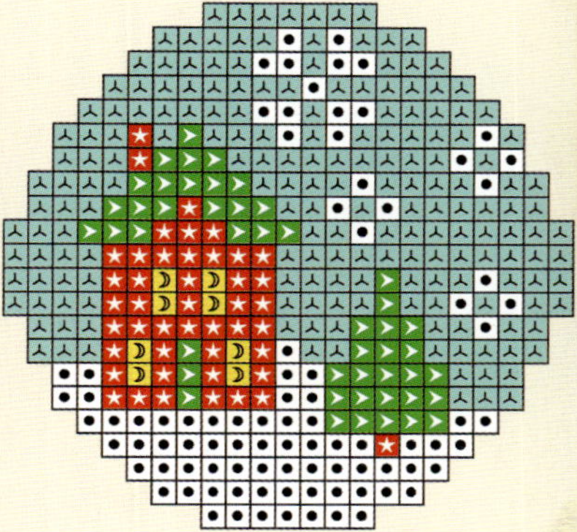

# CHRISTMAS TREE

# MERRY WREATH

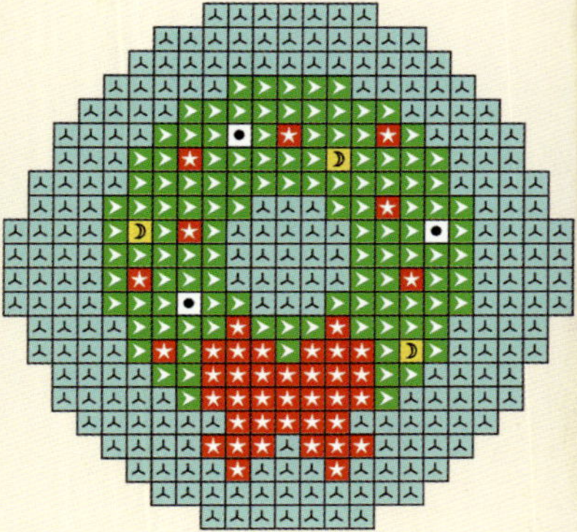

# STRIPEY STOCKING

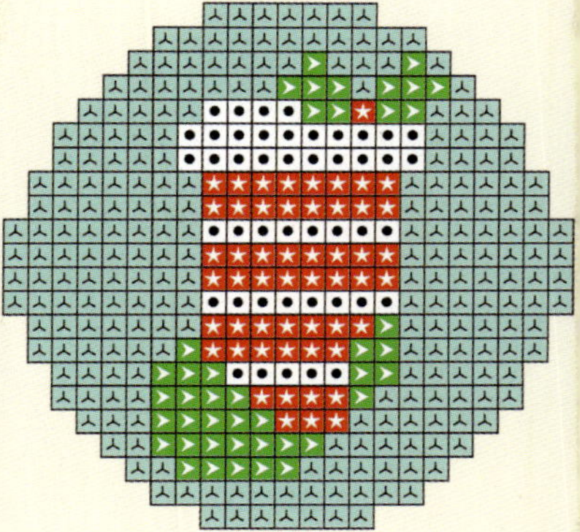

# JOY

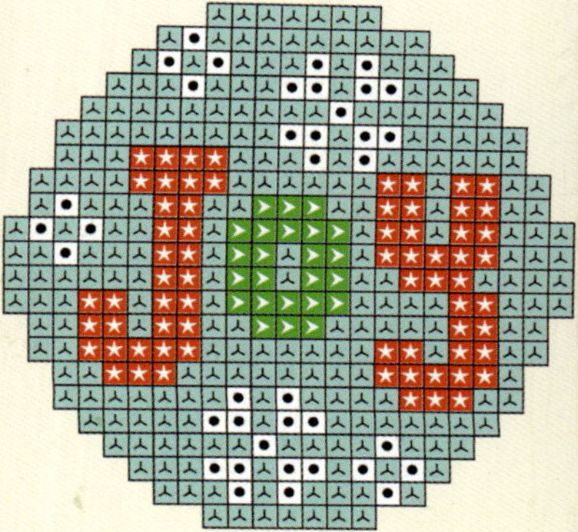